Social Security Benefits Guide (2025)

Everything You Need to Know About Maximizing Your Benefits, Understanding Your Options, and Securing Financial Independence in Retirement

Hart Hawke

TABLE OF CONTENTS

Introduction

Social Security stands as one of the most significant and impactful government programs in the United States, touching the lives of millions of Americans every year. Established in 1935 under President Franklin D. Roosevelt's New Deal, Social Security was designed to provide financial security for retirees, the disabled, and survivors of deceased workers. Over the decades, it has evolved into a lifeline that millions of Americans depend on for financial stability and support during their most vulnerable times. Despite its importance, the program is often misunderstood, misrepresented, and surrounded by myths. This guide aims to clarify its complexities, offering readers a clear understanding of how to maximize their benefits and plan for a secure financial future.

At its core, Social Security functions as a social insurance program funded through payroll taxes under the Federal Insurance Contributions Act (FICA). Every paycheck contributes to this safety net, ensuring that workers and their families have access to income in retirement, during periods of disability, or after the loss of a loved one. While the program was initially created to address the economic hardships of the Great Depression, it has since become an indispensable part of the American social fabric, adapting to meet the needs of a changing society.

Understanding Social Security is essential for anyone planning their financial future. From determining eligibility to choosing the right time to claim benefits, the decisions you make can significantly impact your financial well-being. The program's rules and provisions are complex, but they are designed with the goal of balancing fairness and sustainability. For example, benefits are calculated based on your average earnings over the highest 35 years of your working career. This ensures that those who have contributed more to the system receive larger payouts, while also providing a safety net for low-income workers.

In recent years, Social Security has been at the center of political and economic debates. Questions about the program's solvency, the role of Cost-of-Living Adjustments (COLA), and proposals for reform have become hot-button issues. According to the Social Security Administration (SSA), the trust fund reserves are projected to deplete in the next decade unless Congress takes action to address the shortfall. This looming challenge highlights the importance of understanding how the system works and what changes might lie ahead.

Moreover, the program is not just for retirees. Social Security provides vital support to disabled workers and their families, widows and widowers, and even children. Despite its wide-reaching impact, many Americans are unaware of the benefits they are entitled to or how to access them. This lack of knowledge can lead to missed opportunities and financial hardship, particularly for those who rely heavily on Social Security as their primary source of income.

This guide was created to demystify Social Security, providing readers with actionable insights and practical advice. Whether you are nearing retirement, navigating disability benefits, or simply planning for the future, understanding the nuances of this program is crucial. The chapters ahead will explore everything from the history and evolution of Social Security to strategies for maximizing your benefits.

As we delve into these topics, it is important to approach Social Security with a mindset of empowerment. Knowledge is a powerful tool, and by gaining a deeper understanding of the program, you can make informed decisions that align with your financial goals. With the right strategies, Social Security can serve as a cornerstone of your retirement plan, providing the stability and peace of mind you deserve after a lifetime of hard work.

In the following chapters, we will break down the complexities of Social Security into clear, actionable steps. By the end of this book, you will have a comprehensive understanding of how to navigate the system, claim the benefits you are entitled to, and secure your financial independence. Let this guide be your companion as you explore the opportunities Social Security offers and plan for a brighter, more secure future.

This introduction sets the stage for a detailed and thorough exploration of Social Security. Whether you are a seasoned professional seeking advanced insights or someone entirely new to the topic, this guide will provide the knowledge and tools you need to make the most of this vital program.

Chapter 1
The Evolution of Social Security: A Historical Overview

The history of Social Security in the United States is a story deeply interwoven with the economic, political, and social transformations that have shaped the nation. It stands as one of the most significant federal programs, a cornerstone of the country's social safety net, and a testament to the power of collective responsibility in addressing societal needs.

The origins of Social Security can be traced back to the early 20th century, a period marked by rapid industrialization, urbanization, and economic change. During this time, many Americans faced significant financial insecurity in old age. Families often relied on personal savings, charity, or their children to support them once they could no longer work. However, the stock market crash of 1929 and the Great Depression brought these vulnerabilities into sharp relief. The economic collapse left millions unemployed and destitute, and the elderly, who were often the most vulnerable, suffered greatly.

In response to the widespread economic turmoil, President Franklin D. Roosevelt introduced the New Deal, a series of programs designed to provide relief, recovery, and reform to the American economy. Among these was the Social Security Act of 1935, a landmark piece of legislation that laid the foundation for the Social Security program we know today. The Act established two key programs: Old-Age Insurance, which provided retirement benefits to workers, and Unemployment Insurance, designed to offer temporary financial assistance to those out of work.

The Social Security Act was revolutionary in its scope and ambition. It marked the first time the federal government took on a significant role in ensuring financial security for retired Americans. The program was funded through payroll taxes, with contributions from both employers and employees. This design created a self-sustaining system, where workers essentially funded their own future benefits while also supporting current retirees.

Over the decades, the Social Security program evolved to address the changing needs of American society. In 1939, the program expanded to include benefits for survivors of deceased workers and dependents of retired workers, recognizing the importance of supporting families. This addition made Social Security a broader safety net for millions of Americans.

The 1950s saw further growth, as coverage was extended to millions of additional workers, including farmers, domestic workers, and self-employed individuals. This expansion reflected the shifting labor landscape and ensured that more Americans could participate in and benefit from the program. During the same period, the first cost-of-living adjustment (COLA) was introduced, providing beneficiaries with periodic increases to account for inflation.

In 1965, another major milestone was achieved with the introduction of Medicare, a health insurance program for seniors. Medicare was integrated into Social Security as part of President Lyndon B. Johnson's Great Society initiative. This expansion addressed the rising healthcare costs that often burdened older Americans and further solidified Social Security's role in providing comprehensive support to retirees.

Throughout the 1970s and 1980s, additional amendments were made to the program. These included automatic COLAs, which ensured that benefits kept pace with inflation, and measures to address funding challenges. The Social Security Amendments of 1983, signed into law by President Ronald Reagan, represented a bipartisan effort to stabilize the program's finances. These amendments increased the retirement age, adjusted payroll taxes, and introduced taxation of benefits for higher-income recipients.

Despite its successes, Social Security has faced challenges over the years. The program's financial health is tied to demographic shifts, such as the aging population and declining birth rates. The Baby Boomer generation, in particular, placed significant strain on the system as they began to retire in large numbers. Policymakers have grappled with how to ensure the program's long-term solvency while maintaining its commitment to beneficiaries.

In recent years, debates over Social Security have intensified, with proposals ranging from privatization to benefit expansion. Advocates for expansion argue that Social Security is more critical than ever, given the erosion of traditional pensions and the growing reliance on defined-contribution plans like 401(k)s. Meanwhile, critics warn of the program's impending insolvency and call for reforms to reduce costs and increase sustainability.

Despite these challenges, Social Security remains a cornerstone of American life. It has lifted millions out of poverty, provided a reliable income for retirees, and offered critical support to disabled individuals and families. The program's endurance is a testament to its foundational principles: that a society should provide for its most vulnerable members and ensure dignity in old age.

The evolution of Social Security reflects the United States' ongoing effort to balance individual responsibility with collective support. It is a program shaped by the needs and values of its people, and its history offers valuable lessons about the power of shared investment in the common good. As the nation continues to grapple with questions about the program's future, Social Security's legacy remains a powerful reminder of its impact on the lives of millions of Americans.

Chapter 2
Understanding How Social Security Works

Social Security is one of the most critical components of the American social safety net. Established in 1935 during the Great Depression, it was designed to provide financial security for older Americans who could no longer work, as well as for individuals with disabilities and families of deceased workers. Understanding how Social Security works is essential for anyone planning their financial future, as it affects millions of lives in the United States.

At its core, Social Security is a federal program funded primarily through payroll taxes under the Federal Insurance Contributions Act (FICA). Employers and employees each contribute 6.2% of an employee's earnings, up to a taxable maximum amount, which is adjusted annually. Self-employed individuals pay 12.4% of their earnings to account for both the employer and employee shares. These taxes go into two trust funds: the Old-Age and Survivors Insurance (OASI) Trust Fund and the Disability Insurance (DI) Trust Fund. Together, these funds ensure benefits are paid to eligible individuals.

Social Security functions as a "pay-as-you-go" system, meaning that the taxes collected from current workers and employers are used to pay benefits to current retirees, disabled workers, and their families. While this may seem straightforward, the system is built on a complex formula that takes into account an individual's earnings history, age of retirement, and specific eligibility requirements.

To qualify for Social Security benefits, an individual must earn "credits" by working and paying Social Security taxes. In 2024, for example, a worker earns one credit for every $1,640 in covered earnings, up to a maximum of four credits per year. Most workers need 40 credits, or about 10 years of work, to qualify for retirement benefits. For disability benefits, the credit requirements vary depending on the age at which the disability occurs.

The amount of benefits received is calculated using a worker's average indexed monthly earnings (AIME) over their 35 highest-earning years. The Social Security Administration (SSA) applies a formula to this average to determine the primary insurance amount (PIA), which is the benefit a worker would receive if they retired at their full retirement age

(FRA). The FRA varies depending on the year of birth; for most Americans born after 1960, it is 67 years old.

While full benefits are available at FRA, individuals can choose to claim benefits as early as age 62, but this comes with a reduction in monthly payments. For example, claiming benefits at age 62 could reduce monthly payments by as much as 30% compared to waiting until FRA. Conversely, delaying benefits beyond FRA can result in increased payments due to delayed retirement credits, up to age 70. Each year of delay increases benefits by approximately 8%, providing a significant incentive for those who can afford to wait.

Social Security is not just for retirees. It provides essential financial support for disabled individuals who meet the program's strict criteria. The Disability Insurance (DI) component offers benefits to workers who can no longer perform substantial gainful activity due to a qualifying medical condition expected to last at least one year or result in death. Additionally, Social Security offers survivor benefits to families of deceased workers, including minor children, disabled dependents, and surviving spouses.

Another critical feature of Social Security is its progressive benefit formula, designed to replace a higher percentage of income for lower earners than for higher earners. This structure ensures that the program serves as a lifeline for millions of Americans who depend on it for their basic needs.

It's important to note that Social Security benefits are subject to taxation under certain conditions. If an individual's combined income—which includes adjusted gross income, nontaxable interest, and half of their Social Security benefits—exceeds specific thresholds, up to 85% of their benefits may be taxable. This aspect often catches beneficiaries by surprise and highlights the importance of financial planning.

Social Security faces ongoing challenges, including demographic shifts and financial sustainability. As the U.S. population ages and birth rates decline, fewer workers are contributing to the system relative to the number of beneficiaries. The Social Security Trustees project that, without legislative changes, the trust funds could be depleted by 2033, at which point incoming payroll taxes would only cover approximately 77% of scheduled benefits. While this scenario does not mean the program would cease to exist, it underscores the urgency for reforms to ensure long-term solvency.

For many Americans, Social Security represents a significant portion of their retirement income. However, it was never intended to be the sole source of support. Beneficiaries are encouraged to complement Social Security with personal savings, employer-sponsored retirement plans, and other income sources to achieve financial security in retirement.

Understanding Social Security's intricacies is crucial for making informed decisions about when to claim benefits, how to maximize payouts, and how to integrate Social Security into a broader financial plan. It's a program that continues to evolve, shaped by economic, political, and demographic forces, but its role as a cornerstone of financial stability for millions of Americans remains steadfast.

Chapter 3
Eligibility Requirements: Are You Covered?

Social Security benefits are a cornerstone of financial security for millions of Americans, but not everyone is automatically eligible to receive them. Understanding the eligibility requirements is essential for ensuring you receive the benefits you've earned. These requirements are based on factors such as your work history, age, and type of benefit you are applying for. This chapter will provide a clear, in-depth explanation of what it takes to qualify for Social Security benefits and what steps you can take to confirm your eligibility.

To qualify for Social Security benefits, the fundamental requirement is that you or someone in your family, such as a spouse or parent, must have worked in a job covered by Social Security and paid into the system through payroll taxes, also known as FICA (Federal Insurance Contributions Act) taxes. Each year you work and pay these taxes, you earn "credits" that count toward your eligibility. The credits represent your contribution to the Social Security system, essentially funding your future benefits.

In 2025, the system requires you to earn 40 credits to qualify for most Social Security retirement benefits. You can earn up to four credits per year. Each credit corresponds to a specific amount of earnings, which is adjusted annually to account for inflation. For instance, in 2024, one credit was earned for every $1,640 of income, and this threshold is expected to increase slightly for 2025. For most people, earning 40 credits means working approximately ten years in jobs covered by Social Security. However, if you stop working before earning the necessary credits, you may not be eligible for benefits unless you return to covered employment later.

It's worth noting that not all jobs are covered by Social Security. Federal employees hired before 1984, certain state and local government employees, and some railroad workers participate in separate retirement systems and may not pay into Social Security. These individuals may be subject to specific provisions, such as the Windfall Elimination Provision (WEP) or Government Pension Offset (GPO), which could affect their eligibility and benefit amounts.

For those applying for Social Security disability benefits (SSDI), the work credit requirements differ based on age. Younger workers may qualify with fewer credits, reflecting the fact that they haven't had as much time to accumulate a full work history. For example, a worker under the age of 24 may qualify with as few as six credits earned in the three years leading up to their disability. The rules for survivors' benefits are similarly distinct, with credits calculated based on the deceased worker's age and work history.

Another crucial aspect of eligibility is your age. For retirement benefits, you can begin receiving Social Security as early as age 62. However, applying before your full retirement age—currently between 66 and 67, depending on your birth year—will result in a reduced monthly payment. Conversely, delaying benefits past your full retirement age can increase your payout through delayed retirement credits, which accumulate until age 70.

For spousal and survivor benefits, eligibility hinges on your relationship to the worker and, in some cases, your own age and marital status. For example, a surviving spouse is generally eligible for benefits at age 60 (or age 50 if disabled), while a spouse caring for a child under 16 may qualify at any age. Divorced spouses may also be eligible for benefits if their marriage lasted at least ten years and they meet other criteria.

An often-overlooked factor in eligibility is legal residency status. Social Security benefits are available to U.S. citizens and certain categories of noncitizens, including lawful permanent residents and some nonresidents with sufficient work credits earned in the United States. If you're not a U.S. citizen, additional rules may apply, such as restrictions on receiving benefits while living outside the country.

It's essential to verify your eligibility status early to avoid surprises when you apply. You can do this by creating a "my Social Security" account on the official Social Security Administration (SSA) website. This account allows you to review your earnings history, calculate your expected benefits, and confirm whether you have met the credit requirements for eligibility. If you notice discrepancies in your earnings record, it's vital to correct them promptly by contacting the SSA and providing documentation such as W-2 forms or tax returns.

Moreover, understanding the nuances of eligibility requirements can help you plan your work and retirement strategies more effectively. For instance, if you're nearing the 40-credit threshold but considering early retirement, working a few more years to secure your eligibility could significantly impact your financial stability in retirement. Similarly, if you're a noncitizen or a worker in a noncovered job, exploring alternative strategies, such as qualifying for benefits through a spouse's work history, may be beneficial.

Social Security eligibility is determined by a combination of factors, including work credits, age, and the specific type of benefit being sought. While the rules can seem complex, taking the time to understand and confirm your eligibility can make a significant difference in your financial planning. Whether you're nearing retirement, managing a disability, or planning for survivors' benefits, knowing the requirements ensures that you can access the safety net you've contributed to throughout your working life.

Chapter 4
Maximizing Your Retirement Benefits

Maximizing your retirement benefits is not only about knowing the numbers but also about crafting a strategy that works for your unique circumstances. Social Security plays a crucial role in ensuring financial security during retirement, and understanding how to optimize it can significantly impact your long-term financial well-being. This chapter will delve into actionable steps, key considerations, and strategic choices that can help you maximize the value of your Social Security benefits.

One of the most critical decisions retirees face is determining the right time to claim their benefits. Social Security benefits can be claimed as early as age 62, but doing so results in a permanent reduction in monthly payouts. On the other hand, delaying benefits beyond your full retirement age (FRA)—which is typically between 66 and 67, depending on your birth year—can increase your monthly benefit amount by 8% for each year you delay, up until age 70. This means that if you can afford to wait, you could potentially receive a significantly higher payout over the course of your retirement.

For many individuals, the decision about when to claim benefits should be based on a combination of factors, including current financial needs, life expectancy, and employment status. If you are still working past your FRA, delaying benefits can allow you to maximize your Social Security income while avoiding the earnings test, which reduces benefits for those under FRA who earn above a certain threshold. Additionally, if you have a family history of longevity or are in good health, waiting to claim benefits may be a financially sound decision.

Understanding the impact of spousal and survivor benefits is another way to maximize your retirement income. For married couples, one spouse can claim benefits based on the other's work record, provided it results in a higher benefit. Spousal benefits can be as much as 50% of the higher-earning spouse's benefit, and this option is particularly beneficial for individuals who may not have earned sufficient credits through their own work history. Furthermore, if one spouse passes away, the surviving spouse is entitled to receive the higher of the two benefits.

Planning around these provisions can ensure that your household maximizes Social Security payouts over time.

Another strategy involves coordinating benefits with other sources of retirement income. Social Security is designed to replace approximately 40% of pre-retirement income for the average worker, which means it is most effective when supplemented by pensions, savings, or investments. Retirees who plan their withdrawals strategically can minimize their tax liabilities and ensure their benefits go further. For example, withdrawing from tax-advantaged accounts like a Roth IRA may help reduce the portion of Social Security benefits subject to taxation. Understanding how benefits interact with other income streams is essential for maximizing overall retirement resources.

It is also important to stay informed about cost-of-living adjustments (COLA). Social Security benefits are adjusted annually based on inflation to preserve purchasing power. While these adjustments help offset the rising cost of living, they are not guaranteed to keep pace with all expenses, particularly healthcare costs, which tend to rise faster than general inflation. Retirees should account for these factors when planning their budgets and should consider supplemental strategies, such as investing in healthcare savings accounts or long-term care insurance, to cover gaps.

For individuals impacted by the Windfall Elimination Provision (WEP) or the Government Pension Offset (GPO), understanding how these rules affect benefits is crucial. These provisions reduce Social Security payouts for certain public-sector employees who also receive pensions from non-Social Security-covered work. While these reductions can be substantial, being proactive about understanding the implications and seeking expert advice can help mitigate their impact. Additionally, recent legislative efforts to repeal or reform these provisions may create opportunities for increased benefits in the future.

Lastly, vigilance is key to maximizing benefits. Retirees should regularly review their Social Security statements to ensure earnings are accurately recorded. Mistakes in reported income can lead to reduced benefits, so correcting errors promptly is essential. Using the Social Security Administration's online tools, such as the mySocialSecurity account, can help retirees monitor their records, estimate future benefits, and explore different claiming scenarios.

Chapter 5
Claiming Benefits: When and How to Apply

Claiming Social Security benefits is a significant step in planning for retirement and financial security. Understanding the timing and process involved can maximize the benefits you receive, aligning them with your financial goals and long-term plans. This chapter provides a detailed, step-by-step explanation of when and how to apply for Social Security benefits, ensuring you are well-prepared to make informed decisions.

The first step in claiming your benefits is determining the right time to apply. Social Security offers flexibility in this regard, allowing individuals to start receiving benefits as early as age 62 or delay claiming until age 70. Your decision will directly impact the amount of your monthly benefit. Claiming benefits before your full retirement age (FRA) results in a reduced payout, while delaying beyond FRA can increase your benefits through delayed retirement credits. Full retirement age varies depending on your birth year; for those born in 1960 or later, it is 67.

To make the best decision, consider factors such as your current financial needs, life expectancy, health, and whether you plan to continue working. If you need immediate income or have health concerns, claiming early may make sense, despite the reduced payout. However, if you can afford to wait and anticipate living a long life, delaying your claim will provide a larger monthly benefit, which can significantly enhance your financial security in later years.

Once you've decided on the right time to apply, the process of claiming benefits is straightforward and user-friendly. The Social Security Administration (SSA) offers multiple application methods to accommodate various preferences and accessibility needs. You can apply online through the official SSA website, by phone, or in person at a local Social Security office. The online application process is the most convenient for many people, allowing you to complete the process from the comfort of your home.

Before starting the application process, gather all necessary documents and information to ensure a smooth experience. You will need your Social Security number, birth certificate, proof of U.S. citizenship or lawful residency if not born in the U.S., and military discharge papers if applicable. Additionally, have your banking information ready if you wish to set up direct deposit for your benefits.

The online application process involves creating or logging into your mySocialSecurity account. From there, follow the step-by-step prompts to enter your personal information, work history, and benefit preferences. The system allows you to save your progress, making it easy to complete the application at your own pace. Applying by phone or in person follows a similar procedure but may require scheduling an appointment in advance, especially for in-office visits.

After submitting your application, the SSA will review your information to ensure accuracy and eligibility. This process may take a few weeks, during which you may be asked to provide additional documentation or clarification. Once approved, you will receive a notification outlining your benefit amount and the date your payments will begin. Payments are typically issued monthly and can be received via direct deposit or paper check, though direct deposit is strongly encouraged for its speed and reliability.

It's also important to understand the implications of continuing to work while claiming benefits. If you claim Social Security before reaching your full retirement age and continue to earn income, your benefits may be temporarily reduced based on the SSA's earnings limit. In 2024, this limit is $21,240 annually, and benefits are reduced by $1 for every $2 earned over the threshold. However, once you reach your full retirement age, the earnings limit no longer applies, and your benefits are recalculated to account for any previously withheld amounts.

For those nearing retirement, the decision of when and how to claim benefits can seem daunting. To make the most informed choice, consider consulting a financial advisor or utilizing tools like the SSA's Retirement Estimator. These resources can provide personalized projections of your benefits based on your earnings history and anticipated retirement age.

Chapter 6
Social Security for Spouses, Widows, and Survivors

Social Security isn't just a program for retirees or disabled workers—it also plays a critical role in providing financial security for spouses, widows, and survivors. These benefits aim to ensure that family members who depend on a worker's income aren't left without support when life's uncertainties strike. Understanding how Social Security works for these groups can empower families to make informed decisions and maximize their benefits.

For spouses, Social Security offers benefits based on either their own work record or that of their partner, whichever is higher. A spouse can begin receiving benefits as early as age 62, provided the primary worker has already filed for their benefits. The spousal benefit can be as much as 50% of the working spouse's full retirement age (FRA) benefit. This is particularly valuable for those who may have worked part-time, had lower-paying jobs, or spent years out of the workforce raising a family.

However, timing is crucial. If a spouse claims benefits before reaching their own FRA, the amount will be reduced permanently. For instance, if someone claims at 62 instead of their FRA, their spousal benefit could be significantly less. Conversely, waiting until FRA ensures they receive the maximum spousal benefit available. It's important to note that spousal benefits do not increase if they are delayed beyond FRA, unlike worker benefits.

Widows and widowers have additional considerations. When a worker passes away, their spouse may be eligible for survivor benefits, which can equal 100% of the deceased worker's benefit if the survivor has reached their own FRA. If the survivor chooses to claim benefits earlier, they will receive a reduced amount, but this option can be critical for families who need financial support immediately after the loss of a loved one. Survivor benefits can begin as early as age 60, or even age 50 if the surviving spouse is disabled.

For surviving spouses with dependent children under the age of 16, there are added benefits. They may qualify for survivor benefits regardless of age, helping to support families during challenging transitions.

Additionally, unmarried children under 18, or up to 19 if still in high school, can receive benefits based on the deceased parent's record, further underscoring the program's importance to family stability.

Social Security also provides benefits to divorced spouses under certain conditions. A divorced spouse may claim spousal or survivor benefits if the marriage lasted at least 10 years, they remain unmarried (in most cases), and they meet age and eligibility requirements. Divorced spouses are entitled to the same benefits as current spouses, without reducing the benefits paid to the worker or their current spouse.

For many families, survivor benefits can act as a financial lifeline. When a household loses one of its primary earners, the continuation of Social Security benefits ensures that widows, widowers, and their children can maintain a sense of economic stability. However, it's vital to strategize how and when to claim these benefits to maximize the total lifetime payout. For example, delaying the claim to survivor benefits until FRA often results in higher monthly payments, which can make a significant difference over time.

Navigating Social Security benefits for spouses, widows, and survivors involves understanding the nuances of eligibility, timing, and payout structures. For instance, widows and widowers may choose to claim survivor benefits first while delaying their own retirement benefits to grow through delayed retirement credits. This strategy can result in a larger overall payout.

It's also essential to stay informed about changes in legislation or adjustments to the program, as these could impact eligibility or benefit amounts. Tools like the Social Security Administration's (SSA) online calculators and resources are invaluable for estimating benefits and planning for the future.

Chapter 7
Navigating Disability Benefits

Navigating Social Security Disability Benefits can be a complex process, but understanding the system is essential for those who rely on it for financial support. Social Security Disability Insurance (SSDI) and Supplemental Security Income (SSI) are two key programs that provide assistance to individuals unable to work due to a disabling condition. These programs are vital lifelines for millions of Americans, ensuring that they can meet their basic needs despite significant health challenges.

The first step to accessing Social Security Disability benefits is determining eligibility. The Social Security Administration (SSA) has strict criteria that must be met to qualify for benefits. For SSDI, applicants must have worked and paid Social Security taxes for a certain period, earning sufficient "work credits." Typically, an individual needs to have worked for five of the last ten years before becoming disabled. The severity of the disability is also a crucial factor; the SSA requires that the condition must be severe enough to prevent the individual from engaging in any substantial gainful activity (SGA) and is expected to last at least 12 months or result in death.

SSI, on the other hand, is designed for individuals with limited income and resources, regardless of their work history. To qualify, applicants must demonstrate financial need, in addition to meeting the medical criteria for a disabling condition. Unlike SSDI, SSI is funded by general tax revenues and not by Social Security taxes, making it an option for those who do not have a sufficient work history.

The application process for disability benefits can be challenging, requiring detailed documentation of medical conditions, work history, and financial status. Applicants are required to provide comprehensive medical evidence, including physician statements, test results, and treatment records, to prove the existence and severity of the disability. The SSA evaluates this evidence against their official Listing of Impairments, a comprehensive guide of conditions that automatically qualify for benefits if the criteria are met. If an applicant's condition is not listed, the SSA considers their residual functional capacity (RFC) to determine if they can perform any other type of work.

Despite the thorough preparation required, many applications are denied on the first attempt, often due to incomplete documentation or failure to meet the SSA's strict definitions. Applicants have the right to appeal a denial, and the appeals process typically involves multiple stages, including reconsideration, hearings before an administrative law judge, and, if necessary, review by the Appeals Council or federal court. Persistence and proper legal representation can significantly increase the chances of success during the appeals process.

Disability benefits provide not only monthly financial support but also access to crucial resources such as Medicare or Medicaid. SSDI recipients become eligible for Medicare after a two-year waiting period, while SSI beneficiaries are usually eligible for Medicaid immediately upon approval. These healthcare benefits are invaluable for managing ongoing medical expenses and ensuring continued care for disabling conditions.

For many recipients, returning to work after a period of disability is a goal, and the SSA provides support through its Ticket to Work program. This initiative offers job training, vocational rehabilitation, and other services to help individuals re-enter the workforce without immediately losing their benefits. The SSA also has work incentives, such as the Trial Work Period, which allows beneficiaries to test their ability to work without jeopardizing their SSDI eligibility. These programs aim to empower individuals to achieve financial independence while maintaining a safety net during the transition.

It's important to understand the ongoing responsibilities of receiving disability benefits. Recipients are required to report any changes in their medical condition, income, or work status to the SSA. Periodic reviews, known as Continuing Disability Reviews (CDRs), are conducted to ensure that beneficiaries still meet the eligibility criteria. Failure to comply with these requirements can result in the termination of benefits.

Navigating the Social Security Disability system requires patience, attention to detail, and often professional guidance. Advocacy groups, legal professionals, and nonprofit organizations can provide valuable support throughout the process, from completing the initial application to appealing a denial. The complexity of the system underscores the importance of thorough preparation and persistence for those seeking assistance.

Disability benefits are more than financial support—they represent a vital safety net that allows individuals with significant health challenges to maintain dignity and stability. By understanding the eligibility requirements, application process, and available resources, beneficiaries can navigate this essential program with confidence and clarity, ensuring they receive the support they deserve.

Chapter 8
How the Windfall Elimination Provision (WEP) and Government Pension Offset (GPO) Affect You

The Windfall Elimination Provision (WEP) and the Government Pension Offset (GPO) are two laws that have a profound impact on the Social Security benefits of public-sector workers and their families. While these provisions were introduced with the intention of addressing perceived inequities in the Social Security system, they have often created significant challenges for those who depend on public pensions. Understanding how these provisions work, who they affect, and the broader implications for financial planning is essential for anyone impacted by them.

The **Windfall Elimination Provision (WEP)** adjusts the Social Security benefit formula for individuals who receive a public pension from a job where they did not pay Social Security taxes. It applies primarily to workers in state and local government positions, as well as certain federal positions not covered by Social Security. The idea behind WEP is to ensure that workers with non-covered pensions do not receive what is viewed as disproportionately higher Social Security benefits.

Here's how WEP works: Social Security benefits are calculated based on a worker's average indexed monthly earnings (AIME). The standard formula applies a higher percentage to the first portion of AIME, providing a larger relative benefit for lower-income earners. For workers affected by WEP, this formula is adjusted, effectively reducing the benefits they would otherwise receive. The amount of the reduction depends on the number of years a worker paid Social Security taxes and the size of their public pension. In 2024, the maximum reduction under WEP is capped at $600 per month.

Critics of WEP argue that it penalizes workers who have earned both Social Security credits and a public pension, disproportionately impacting educators, police officers, firefighters, and other public servants. For example, an individual who worked for 15 years in a private sector job and then transitioned to a teaching position covered by a public pension might find their Social Security benefits significantly reduced due to WEP. This creates confusion and frustration for retirees who may not have been fully aware of these implications when planning their careers and finances.

The **Government Pension Offset (GPO)**, on the other hand, affects spousal and survivor benefits. It applies to individuals who receive a government pension from non-Social Security-covered work and are also eligible for Social Security spousal or survivor benefits. Unlike WEP, which modifies the benefit formula, GPO reduces Social Security benefits by two-thirds of the amount of the government pension.

For example, if a retired public servant receives a monthly government pension of $3,000, their spousal or survivor Social Security benefit would be reduced by $2,000 (two-thirds of the pension amount). This can lead to cases where retirees receive little to no spousal or survivor benefit, even though their spouses paid into Social Security for decades.

Supporters of GPO argue that it prevents individuals from "double-dipping" by receiving full benefits from both a public pension and Social Security. However, opponents contend that GPO unfairly targets lower-income public-sector retirees and their families, often leaving widows and widowers in financially precarious situations.

Together, WEP and GPO have been a source of significant controversy. Proponents maintain that these provisions uphold the integrity of the Social Security system by addressing potential inequities. However, detractors argue that the rules are overly punitive and fail to account for the diverse career paths and financial realities of modern workers. Many affected individuals believe that the provisions create unintended inequities, particularly for those who have split their careers between covered and non-covered employment.

In response to these concerns, there have been numerous efforts in Congress to reform or repeal WEP and GPO. Most recently, legislation has been introduced to repeal these provisions, with strong bipartisan support. Advocates for repeal highlight stories of public servants who face severe financial hardships due to reduced Social Security benefits. They argue that these provisions disproportionately hurt individuals who have dedicated their careers to serving the public, such as teachers, nurses, and first responders.

However, the financial implications of repealing WEP and GPO are significant. According to the Congressional Budget Office (CBO), eliminating these provisions would add billions of dollars to the federal deficit and accelerate the insolvency of the Social Security trust fund. This creates a difficult balancing act for policymakers who must weigh the financial sustainability of the Social Security system against the immediate needs of affected retirees.

For individuals impacted by WEP or GPO, understanding these provisions is critical for effective financial planning. Retirees should review their Social Security statements carefully and consult with financial advisors to anticipate the effects of these provisions on their retirement income. Awareness and proactive planning can help mitigate the financial impact and ensure a more stable retirement.

WEP and GPO highlight the complexities of the Social Security system and the challenges of ensuring fairness while maintaining long-term solvency. As debates over these provisions continue, it remains to be seen whether reforms will address the concerns of those affected without jeopardizing the financial stability of the program as a whole.

Chapter 9
The Role of Cost-of-Living Adjustments (COLA)

Cost-of-Living Adjustments (COLA) are an essential feature of the Social Security program, designed to ensure that beneficiaries maintain their purchasing power as inflation rises over time. Without COLA, the fixed payments from Social Security would lose value year after year, leaving retirees, disabled individuals, and survivors unable to keep up with the increasing costs of everyday necessities such as food, housing, and healthcare. This chapter will explain how COLA works, its calculation method, its impact on beneficiaries, and the broader implications for the Social Security system.

At its core, COLA is a mechanism that ties Social Security benefits to the Consumer Price Index for Urban Wage Earners and Clerical Workers (CPI-W). The CPI-W is a measure of inflation that tracks changes in the prices of goods and services commonly purchased by working households. Each year, the Social Security Administration (SSA) examines the CPI-W data from the third quarter (July through September) and compares it to the corresponding period from the previous year. If there is an increase in the CPI-W, Social Security benefits are adjusted upward by the percentage of that increase. This ensures that benefits remain aligned with the cost of living.

COLA adjustments typically take effect in January of the following year, impacting more than 70 million Americans who rely on Social Security or Supplemental Security Income (SSI). The size of the adjustment varies from year to year, reflecting the unpredictable nature of inflation. For example, during periods of high inflation, COLA increases can be substantial, as seen in 2023, when beneficiaries received a 5.9% adjustment—the largest in decades. Conversely, during periods of low inflation or deflation, COLA may be minimal or even nonexistent, as occurred in 2010, 2011, and 2016.

For beneficiaries, COLA plays a critical role in safeguarding their financial security. Retirees, who form the majority of Social Security recipients, often live on fixed incomes and are especially vulnerable to rising costs. COLA ensures they can continue affording essentials such as groceries, utilities, and medications. Similarly, disabled workers and their families, as well as survivors of deceased workers, benefit from COLA adjustments that help them cope with the financial challenges of inflation.

However, while COLA is a lifeline for many, it is not without its limitations. Critics argue that the CPI-W does not accurately reflect the spending patterns of Social Security recipients, particularly retirees. For instance, retirees tend to spend a larger share of their income on healthcare, which has historically experienced higher inflation rates than other goods and services. As a result, some advocate for switching to a different inflation index, such as the Consumer Price Index for the Elderly (CPI-E), which more accurately captures the spending habits of older Americans.

Also to its impact on beneficiaries, COLA also has significant implications for the Social Security trust funds. Higher COLA adjustments lead to increased benefit payouts, which can strain the program's finances. With the Social Security trust funds projected to face depletion in the coming decades, larger-than-expected COLA increases can accelerate the timeline for insolvency unless accompanied by higher revenues or other reforms. Policymakers must balance the need to protect beneficiaries from inflation with the imperative to maintain the long-term solvency of the program.

The role of COLA in shaping public perceptions of Social Security cannot be overstated. For many Americans, COLA adjustments are a tangible demonstration of the program's commitment to supporting its beneficiaries. Annual announcements of COLA rates often make headlines and spark debates about the adequacy of benefits, the fairness of the CPI-W as a measure of inflation, and the broader challenges facing the Social Security system.

Chapter 10
Taxation of Social Security Benefits

Social Security benefits provide a financial safety net for millions of retirees, disabled individuals, and their families. However, many people are surprised to discover that their Social Security income may be subject to federal taxation. Understanding how and why Social Security benefits are taxed can help beneficiaries better plan their finances and avoid unexpected surprises. This chapter delves into the nuances of Social Security benefit taxation, equipping readers with the knowledge to navigate this critical aspect of retirement planning.

Social Security benefits became subject to federal taxation in 1984 as part of a reform intended to bolster the program's financial health. Initially, only a small percentage of recipients were affected, but over the years, the thresholds for taxation have remained unchanged despite inflation and rising income levels. As a result, a growing number of beneficiaries now find their benefits subject to tax.

The taxation of Social Security benefits depends on a calculation known as "combined income," also referred to as "provisional income." Combined income is calculated by adding the following:

- Your adjusted gross income (AGI)
- Nontaxable interest, such as income from municipal bonds
- 50% of your annual Social Security benefits

The outcome of this calculation determines whether your benefits are taxable and to what extent. The IRS has established two key thresholds to assess taxation:

1. If you file as an individual and your combined income is between $25,000 and $34,000, up to 50% of your Social Security benefits may be taxable. If your combined income exceeds $34,000, up to 85% of your benefits may be subject to taxation.
2. For those filing jointly, if combined income is between $32,000 and $44,000, up to 50% of benefits may be taxable. If combined income surpasses $44,000, up to 85% of benefits may be taxed.

It's important to note that these thresholds are not adjusted for inflation, meaning more beneficiaries are taxed each year as income levels rise. This "bracket creep" has sparked debate over whether the thresholds should be revised to reflect current economic realities.

The tax rate applied to taxable Social Security benefits corresponds to the federal income tax bracket of the individual or couple. For example, if a beneficiary's taxable income places them in the 22% bracket, that rate will apply to the taxable portion of their benefits. Importantly, no more than 85% of a recipient's Social Security benefits are ever subject to federal taxation, regardless of income level.

In addition to federal taxes, some states also tax Social Security benefits. Currently, 12 states impose taxes on Social Security income, though the rules vary widely. States like Colorado and Connecticut offer deductions or exemptions based on income, while others apply taxes uniformly. Beneficiaries living in these states should carefully review their local tax laws to understand the impact on their benefits.

There are strategies to minimize the taxation of Social Security benefits. One common approach is to manage withdrawals from retirement accounts such as IRAs and 401(k)s to control combined income levels. Tax-efficient withdrawals, where taxable income is spread across multiple years, can help keep combined income below the thresholds. Additionally, beneficiaries may consider Roth conversions or using Roth IRAs, as withdrawals from Roth accounts are not included in combined income calculations.

For retirees who depend on Social Security as their primary income source, tax credits and deductions may help offset the financial burden. For example, the Senior Tax Credit, available to those aged 65 or older, can reduce the overall tax liability if eligibility requirements are met. Proper planning and consultation with a financial advisor or tax professional can ensure retirees take full advantage of available tax benefits and minimize the impact of Social Security taxation.

While federal taxation of Social Security benefits is a significant consideration, it is not insurmountable. By understanding the rules and thresholds and employing strategic financial planning, beneficiaries can effectively manage their tax liabilities. This not only preserves more of their hard-earned benefits but also contributes to a more secure and predictable retirement.

As debates continue about reforming Social Security and adjusting taxation thresholds, beneficiaries should stay informed about legislative changes. Proactive planning and knowledge are key to making the most of Social Security benefits while navigating the complexities of taxation.

Chapter 11
Social Security and Medicare: What You Need to Know

Social Security and Medicare are two of the most critical safety net programs in the United States, providing essential financial and healthcare support to millions of Americans. Understanding how these programs work together is vital for ensuring you make the most of your benefits while planning for retirement or managing healthcare needs in later years.

Social Security is primarily a program designed to provide financial assistance to retirees, disabled individuals, and their families. Medicare, on the other hand, is a federal health insurance program that primarily serves people aged 65 and older, as well as certain younger individuals with disabilities or end-stage renal disease. While these programs serve different purposes, they are closely intertwined in the lives of beneficiaries.

The Role of Social Security in Medicare Enrollment

One of the most significant links between Social Security and Medicare is the automatic enrollment process. If you are receiving Social Security benefits when you turn 65, you will typically be automatically enrolled in Medicare Part A (hospital insurance) and Part B (medical insurance). This is a seamless process designed to ensure that retirees have access to healthcare without needing to take extra steps to sign up.

However, if you are not yet receiving Social Security benefits when you turn 65—perhaps because you've delayed claiming them to maximize your monthly payout—you will need to actively enroll in Medicare. Failing to enroll during your Initial Enrollment Period (the seven-month window around your 65th birthday) could result in late enrollment penalties for Part B, which can add significant costs over time.

Medicare Premiums and Social Security Deductions

Many people are surprised to learn that Medicare is not entirely free, even if they have paid into the system through payroll taxes during their working years. Medicare Part A is typically premium-free for those who have worked and paid Social Security taxes for at least 10 years (40 quarters). However, Medicare Part B, which covers outpatient services like doctor visits, diagnostics, and preventive care, comes with a monthly premium.

For most beneficiaries, the cost of Medicare Part B premiums is deducted directly from their Social Security payments. This arrangement makes it easier for retirees to manage their healthcare costs, as they do not need to remember to make separate payments. That said, the exact amount deducted can vary depending on your income. High-income earners may pay higher premiums due to Income-Related Monthly Adjustment Amounts (IRMAA), which are calculated based on your modified adjusted gross income (MAGI) from two years prior.

Medicare Advantage and Prescription Drug Plans

While Original Medicare (Parts A and B) provides comprehensive coverage, it does not cover everything. Many retirees choose to supplement their coverage with either a Medicare Advantage Plan (Part C) or a standalone Prescription Drug Plan (Part D). Social Security plays a role here, too, as premiums for these additional plans can also be deducted directly from your monthly Social Security payment, streamlining the payment process.

Medicare Advantage plans are an alternative to Original Medicare offered by private insurance companies. These plans often bundle Part A, Part B, and Part D coverage and may include extra benefits like dental, vision, or wellness programs. While Medicare Advantage can provide more tailored coverage, it's essential to carefully compare plan options, costs, and provider networks before enrolling.

The Impact of COLA Adjustments on Medicare Costs

Cost-of-Living Adjustments (COLA) are annual increases to Social Security benefits intended to help recipients keep up with inflation. While these adjustments are beneficial, they can sometimes be partially offset by increases in Medicare Part B premiums. This phenomenon is known as the "hold harmless" provision, which ensures that Social Security payments do not decrease from one year to the next due to rising Medicare premiums.

However, not all beneficiaries are protected by this provision. For example, individuals who delay Social Security benefits or those subject to IRMAA may still see a significant portion of their COLA eaten up by higher Medicare costs.

Understanding Late Enrollment Penalties

Both Social Security and Medicare operate under rules designed to encourage timely enrollment. Missing key deadlines can result in penalties that last a lifetime. For Medicare Part B, the penalty is a 10% increase in your premium for every 12 months you delay enrollment without having other credible coverage. Similarly, failing to enroll in a Part D prescription drug plan when first eligible can result in a penalty calculated based on the number of months you were without coverage.

These penalties are deducted from your Social Security benefits, reducing your monthly payout. Therefore, understanding enrollment periods and ensuring you take timely action is crucial.

Planning for Long-Term Healthcare Needs

As healthcare costs continue to rise, many retirees find themselves relying on a combination of Medicare and Social Security to manage their financial and medical needs. However, Original Medicare does not cover long-term care, such as stays in a nursing home or extended home healthcare services. This gap in coverage requires retirees to think critically about their financial plans.

Some individuals opt for long-term care insurance, while others may use savings, assets, or Medicaid (if they qualify) to cover these expenses. Regardless of the approach, integrating Social Security and

Medicare benefits into your broader retirement plan is essential to avoid unexpected financial strain.

Challenges and Reforms

Both Social Security and Medicare face long-term funding challenges. Social Security's trust funds are projected to be depleted by the mid-2030s without legislative intervention, while Medicare's Hospital Insurance Trust Fund faces similar solvency issues. These challenges highlight the importance of staying informed about policy changes that could impact benefits in the future.

As lawmakers debate potential reforms, retirees and those approaching retirement must remain proactive in understanding their options and adapting their financial strategies accordingly.

Final Thoughts

Social Security and Medicare are pillars of retirement security, providing financial stability and access to healthcare for millions of Americans. By understanding how these programs interact and taking steps to maximize your benefits, you can ensure a more secure and comfortable retirement.

Knowledge is power, and being informed about these essential programs can make all the difference in achieving financial independence and peace of mind.

Chapter 12
Addressing Common Myths and Misconceptions

Social Security is one of the most discussed and misunderstood government programs in the United States. For decades, myths and misconceptions about how the system works, who it serves, and what it offers have persisted, leaving many Americans uncertain about what to believe. This chapter aims to demystify Social Security by addressing some of the most common myths and explaining the facts in a straightforward and accurate manner.

One of the most pervasive myths about Social Security is that the program is "running out of money." While it is true that Social Security faces financial challenges, particularly as the population ages and more people claim benefits, the idea that it will be completely bankrupt is misleading. Social Security is funded primarily through payroll taxes collected under the Federal Insurance Contributions Act (FICA). As long as workers and employers continue to pay these taxes, the program will continue to generate income. According to the Social Security Administration (SSA), even if the trust funds that supplement the system are depleted, payroll taxes alone could still cover about 77% of scheduled benefits. While adjustments may be necessary to maintain full solvency, Social Security will not simply vanish.

Another widespread misconception is that Social Security is only for retirees. While retirement benefits are a significant part of the program, Social Security also provides crucial support for disabled workers, their families, and survivors of deceased workers. The Disability Insurance (DI) and Survivors Insurance components of the program ensure that individuals who cannot work due to severe health conditions, and families who lose a breadwinner, receive financial support. This comprehensive safety net often goes unnoticed in discussions that focus solely on retirement.

A third myth revolves around the belief that individuals who do not pay into Social Security during their working years are ineligible for benefits. While it is true that most benefits are based on work credits earned through employment covered by Social Security taxes, there are exceptions. Spouses, widows, and widowers can receive benefits based on their partner's earnings record, even if they have never worked in a Social Security-covered job. For example, a stay-at-home parent who has never contributed to the system may still qualify for spousal or survivor benefits.

Some people mistakenly believe that Social Security benefits are tax-free. While this was true in the early days of the program, it no longer applies universally. Depending on your total income level, a portion of your Social Security benefits may be subject to federal income tax. For individuals with combined incomes above a certain threshold—currently $25,000 for single filers or $32,000 for married couples filing jointly—up to 85% of their benefits can be taxed. This is an important consideration for retirees who rely on Social Security as a primary source of income.

Another common misunderstanding is that Social Security provides a generous income that will cover all retirement needs. In reality, Social Security was designed to replace only a portion of a worker's pre-retirement income—typically around 40%. For higher earners, the replacement rate is even lower. This means that Social Security is meant to serve as a foundation for retirement income, supplemented by personal savings, pensions, or other investments.

Relying solely on Social Security could result in financial strain during retirement.

Some critics argue that Social Security is a "handout," a misconception that undermines the program's intent and structure. In truth, Social Security operates as a social insurance program. Workers earn benefits by contributing a portion of their wages through payroll taxes over the course of their careers. These contributions are not optional, and the benefits received are based on a worker's earnings history and the length of their contributions. Social Security is a self-funded program, not a welfare initiative, and it reflects the principle of shared responsibility among citizens.

Another frequently repeated myth is that young people will never receive Social Security benefits. This belief has gained traction among millennials and Gen Z workers, many of whom are skeptical about the program's future solvency. While the program does face funding challenges, these issues can be addressed through policy changes, such as increasing the payroll tax cap, adjusting benefits for higher-income earners, or gradually raising the retirement age. Historically,

Congress has acted to shore up Social Security's finances when needed, and it is likely to do so again.

Some people believe they have no control over their Social Security benefits. While it is true that the program's rules are set by the federal government, individuals have significant influence over how much they ultimately receive. Decisions such as when to claim benefits, whether to continue working, and how to coordinate spousal or survivor benefits can have a substantial impact on the total amount of benefits received. Delaying benefits, for instance, increases the monthly payment, which can result in a higher lifetime payout for those who live longer.

Addressing these myths and misconceptions is crucial for ensuring that Americans have an accurate understanding of Social Security. By dispelling false information and clarifying the facts, individuals can make informed decisions about their benefits and better prepare for retirement. Social Security remains a vital program, but its effectiveness depends on the public's awareness and understanding of how it works. By embracing the truth and rejecting the myths, Americans can ensure that Social Security continues to provide the security and stability it was designed to deliver.

Chapter 13
Proposed Reforms and the Future of Social Security

Social Security has long been a cornerstone of the American social safety net, providing financial support to retirees, disabled individuals, and surviving family members. However, as the program faces ongoing challenges such as funding shortages and demographic shifts, policymakers and experts have put forward numerous proposals to reform the system and ensure its sustainability for future generations.

At the heart of the issue is the looming insolvency of the Social Security Trust Fund. According to the most recent reports from the Social Security Board of Trustees, without intervention, the trust fund reserves are projected to be depleted by the mid-2030s. At that point, the program would only be able to pay about 75–80% of scheduled benefits using ongoing payroll tax revenue. This stark reality has led to a vigorous debate about how best to address the funding gap while maintaining the integrity and effectiveness of Social Security.

One of the most frequently discussed reforms is raising the full retirement age. Currently, the full retirement age is gradually increasing to 67 for those born in 1960 or later. Some policymakers propose further raising the retirement age to 68, 69, or even 70, citing increased life expectancy and improved health among older adults. Proponents argue that this change reflects the modern realities of aging and would significantly reduce the financial strain on the program. However, critics contend that such a move would disproportionately impact lower-income workers and those in physically demanding jobs, who may not have the luxury of delaying retirement.

Another widely debated proposal is adjusting the payroll tax cap. Social Security is funded primarily through payroll taxes, which apply to earnings up to a certain limit—$160,200 in 2023. Earnings above this cap are not taxed for Social Security. Some reform advocates suggest increasing or eliminating this cap, effectively requiring higher-income individuals to contribute more to the program. This measure, often referred to as "scrapping the cap," could substantially increase revenue and delay the trust fund's depletion. Opponents, however, argue that this approach may discourage economic growth or innovation by imposing higher tax burdens on high earners.

Benefit adjustments also play a central role in reform discussions. Proposals to reduce benefits for higher-income retirees, often called "means testing," aim to ensure that Social Security resources are directed toward those who need them most. While this approach could help reduce costs, critics warn that it could undermine the universal nature of Social Security, which has been one of its defining features since its inception.

On the other hand, some policymakers advocate for expanding benefits rather than cutting them. This perspective focuses on strengthening Social Security's role in reducing economic inequality and poverty among older adults. Proposals in this vein include increasing minimum benefits for low-income retirees, providing caregiver credits to individuals who leave the workforce to care for family members, and restoring benefits for public-sector workers affected by the Windfall Elimination Provision (WEP) and Government Pension Offset (GPO). These measures are seen as a way to modernize Social Security to better reflect the changing realities of work and family life.

Another critical aspect of reform is addressing the program's long-term solvency. Beyond raising revenue or adjusting benefits, some proposals seek to diversify the investment strategy of the Social Security Trust Fund. Currently, the fund is invested exclusively in government bonds, which provide stability but relatively low returns. Advocates of investment diversification suggest allocating a portion of the trust fund to equities or other assets to achieve higher returns over time. However, this approach carries risks, as market volatility could threaten the fund's reliability during economic downturns.

In addition to these specific reforms, there is growing recognition of the need for a comprehensive, bipartisan approach to Social Security's challenges. Many experts emphasize that piecemeal changes may not be sufficient to address the program's long-term issues and that a larger, systemic overhaul is required. However, achieving bipartisan consensus has proven difficult, given the political and ideological divides surrounding Social Security.

The future of Social Security is not just a matter of policy; it is also a question of values. The program reflects a collective commitment to ensuring economic security for all Americans, particularly the most vulnerable. As the debate over reforms continues, it will be crucial to strike a balance between fiscal responsibility and social equity. Policymakers must consider not only the program's financial health but also its impact on individuals and families who rely on it as a lifeline.

The path forward for Social Security will depend on the willingness of lawmakers to make difficult decisions and the ability of the American public to engage in meaningful dialogue about the program's future. With the right reforms, Social Security can continue to fulfill its promise for generations to come.

Chapter 14
Tips for Securing Financial Independence Beyond Social Security

Social Security benefits are a critical component of financial stability for millions of retirees, but relying solely on these benefits often isn't enough to maintain a comfortable lifestyle. Financial independence requires a combination of strategic planning, disciplined savings, and an understanding of how to make your money work for you over time. This chapter explores actionable tips to help you secure financial independence beyond what Social Security can provide.

One of the most important steps in achieving financial independence is creating a comprehensive budget. Start by assessing your monthly income, expenses, and any financial obligations you may have, such as loans or outstanding debts. By keeping track of where your money goes, you can identify areas to cut back and redirect those funds toward savings or investments. Budgeting doesn't have to mean sacrificing everything you enjoy—it's about making intentional choices that prioritize your long-term goals.

Equally important is building an emergency fund. Unexpected expenses, such as medical bills or home repairs, can derail even the best-laid financial plans. Experts recommend saving three to six months' worth of living expenses in an accessible account. This fund acts as a financial buffer, allowing you to cover emergencies without dipping into your retirement savings or accruing debt.

Investing is another key pillar of financial independence. Social Security benefits alone cannot generate the returns needed to outpace inflation and support a secure retirement. Consider diversifying your investment portfolio to include a mix of stocks, bonds, mutual funds, and other assets. If you're new to investing, consulting with a financial advisor can help you make informed decisions that align with your risk tolerance and long-term objectives. Starting early allows compound interest to work in your favor, but it's never too late to begin investing.

Retirement accounts like 401(k)s and Individual Retirement Accounts (IRAs) play a crucial role in supplementing Social Security. Contribute to these accounts as consistently as possible, taking advantage of employer matching programs if available. Roth

IRAs, in particular, offer tax advantages that can maximize your savings over time. Even small, regular contributions add up, especially when combined with the power of compounding.

Debt reduction is another cornerstone of financial independence. High-interest debt, such as credit card balances, can quickly erode your savings and leave you financially vulnerable. Focus on paying off these debts systematically, starting with those that carry the highest interest rates. Once your high-interest debts are under control, you can redirect those funds toward building wealth.

Another vital aspect is to carefully consider your housing situation. Housing often represents one of the largest expenses in retirement, and downsizing can free up significant resources. Moving to a smaller home or relocating to an area with a lower cost of living can help reduce monthly expenses and increase your disposable income. For those with substantial home equity, a reverse mortgage may provide an additional source of income in retirement, though it should be approached with caution and professional advice.

Healthcare costs also deserve careful planning. As healthcare expenses tend to rise with age, ensuring that you have adequate insurance coverage and a financial plan to manage medical costs is essential. Health Savings Accounts (HSAs) can be a powerful tool if you are still working, as they offer tax advantages and allow you to save specifically for medical expenses.

Creating multiple streams of income can further enhance financial independence. Whether through part-time work, rental income, or monetizing a hobby, additional income sources can provide flexibility and security. Passive income, such as dividends from investments or royalties, is especially valuable in maintaining your lifestyle without requiring active labor.

Financial literacy is a lifelong journey. Staying informed about personal finance trends, tax laws, and investment strategies empowers you to make smarter decisions. Attend workshops, read books, and engage with credible financial advisors to refine your knowledge and skills. Financial independence isn't just about having money—it's about knowing how to manage and grow it effectively.

Also, consider your legacy and long-term financial goals. Estate planning, including the creation of wills and trusts, ensures that your assets are distributed according to your wishes. This not only protects your loved ones but also gives you peace of mind that your financial independence extends to those who rely on you.

While Social Security benefits provide a foundation for retirement income, achieving true financial independence requires proactive planning and a diversified approach. By budgeting wisely, saving diligently, reducing debt, and investing strategically, you can create a stable financial future that allows you to live comfortably and confidently beyond Social Security.

Chapter 15

The Impact of Legislation on Public-Sector Workers

Social Security legislation has long been a cornerstone of financial security for millions of Americans. Yet, for decades, public-sector workers—such as educators, firefighters, police officers, and other government employees—have faced significant challenges when it comes to accessing the full benefits of the system. This chapter delves into the historical and contemporary legislative changes that have shaped the Social Security experience for these individuals, highlighting both the inequities and recent efforts to address them.

A Historical Overview

Public-sector workers occupy a unique position in the Social Security system. Many state and local government employees are part of public pension plans that are not integrated with Social Security. This arrangement dates back to the program's inception in 1935, when Social Security excluded state and local government workers to avoid federal overreach into state affairs. Over time, however, as the program expanded, certain public-sector workers were included through agreements between state governments and the Social Security Administration. Despite this progress, a significant portion of these workers still fall outside the Social Security system, leaving them reliant on state pension programs.

Two key provisions have further complicated the relationship between public pensions and Social Security benefits: the **Windfall Elimination Provision (WEP)** and the **Government Pension Offset (GPO)**. These provisions were enacted in the 1980s to address perceived inequities in the system but have since drawn widespread criticism for their unintended consequences.

The Windfall Elimination Provision (WEP)

The WEP reduces Social Security benefits for individuals who receive a public pension from employment not covered by Social Security. The rationale behind the provision was to prevent "double-dipping," where an individual could receive full benefits from both a public pension and Social Security without having paid a proportional amount into the latter system. However, critics argue that the WEP disproportionately penalizes public-sector workers, especially those with short careers in public service or those who worked part-time jobs covered by Social Security. The formula used to calculate the reduction often leads to significant financial losses, reducing benefits by as much as $500 per month in some cases. For many retirees, this has meant struggling to maintain financial stability during retirement.

The Government Pension Offset (GPO)

The GPO affects Social Security benefits for spouses, widows, and widowers who receive a public pension. Under this provision, Social Security spousal or survivor benefits are reduced by two-thirds of the public pension amount. In many cases, this reduction entirely eliminates the Social Security benefit, leaving surviving spouses without a critical source of income. For example, a widow who receives a public pension of $1,500 a month could see her Social Security survivor benefits reduced by $1,000, potentially wiping out her eligibility altogether.

The GPO has been widely criticized for its disproportionate impact on lower-income retirees, particularly women, who are more likely to rely on spousal benefits. Many advocates view the provision as punitive and argue that it unfairly penalizes public-sector workers and their families.

Legislative Efforts to Address Inequities

Recent years have seen growing momentum to reform or repeal the WEP and GPO. Public outcry and advocacy efforts from unions, retiree organizations, and individual workers have brought these issues to the forefront of legislative discussions. The most notable effort to date is the **Social Security Fairness Act**, which seeks to eliminate both provisions entirely. This legislation has garnered bipartisan support, reflecting a recognition of the inequities these provisions have created.

In December 2024, the Senate advanced a bill to repeal the WEP and GPO, marking a significant step toward addressing these long-standing inequities. The legislation, which passed with overwhelming bipartisan support, promises to increase Social Security benefits for over 2 million public-sector workers and their families. Advocates of the bill have highlighted its potential to restore financial dignity to retirees who have been unfairly penalized under the current system.

For instance, under the existing provisions, a retired high school teacher in Louisiana—who spent her career shaping young minds—might see her Social Security benefits reduced to a mere fraction of what she earned through private-sector work. The repeal of these provisions would restore her full benefit, acknowledging the contributions she and countless other public-sector workers have made to society.

Financial and Political Challenges

Despite the strong support for reform, critics argue that repealing the WEP and GPO comes with significant fiscal challenges. The Congressional Budget Office (CBO) estimates that eliminating these provisions would add approximately $196 billion to the federal deficit over the next decade. Additionally, opponents contend that the repeal could accelerate the depletion of the Social Security trust fund, potentially undermining the program's long-term solvency.

These financial concerns have sparked debate among lawmakers, with some advocating for offsetting the costs through increased payroll taxes or other adjustments to the Social Security system. Others argue that the federal budget's broader context—now exceeding $6 trillion annually—makes the cost of repeal relatively modest and justifiable in light of the fairness it would bring to public-sector retirees.

The Broader Implications

The repeal of the WEP and GPO would have far-reaching implications not only for public-sector workers but also for the Social Security system as a whole. For many retirees, the change would mean a significant boost in monthly income, alleviating financial strain and reducing poverty rates among elderly populations. Moreover, the repeal could enhance the program's perceived fairness, bolstering public confidence in Social Security at a time when its solvency is a growing concern.

However, the debate over these provisions also underscores broader questions about the program's future. As lawmakers grapple with balancing fairness, fiscal responsibility, and the needs of retirees, the conversation around Social Security is likely to remain a central issue in American politics for years to come.

The impact of legislation on public-sector workers highlights the complexities of balancing equity and sustainability within the Social Security system. While the repeal of the WEP and GPO would represent a monumental step forward for millions of retirees, it also raises important questions about how to ensure the program's long-term viability. As policymakers and advocates continue to navigate these challenges, one thing is clear: the voices of public-sector workers will remain a vital part of the conversation.

Chapter 16
Strategies for Long-Term Benefit Optimization

Optimizing your Social Security benefits requires a strategic approach to planning your retirement and understanding the intricacies of the system. For millions of Americans, Social Security forms a cornerstone of financial stability during retirement. However, without careful planning, you may leave money on the table that could significantly impact your quality of life. This chapter provides practical, actionable strategies to help you maximize your benefits over the long term.

One of the first steps in optimizing Social Security benefits is determining the right age to claim them. While benefits can be claimed as early as age 62, doing so will result in a permanent reduction in monthly payments. Conversely, delaying benefits until after your full retirement age (FRA)—which ranges from 66 to 67, depending on your birth year—can result in an increase of up to 8% annually until age 70. This means that waiting to claim benefits could result in a significantly larger monthly payment, offering greater financial security during your later years. However, this decision should factor in your health, life expectancy, and financial needs.

Understanding the mechanics of spousal and survivor benefits is another key strategy. If you are married, you may be eligible to claim benefits based on your spouse's work history, even if you never worked yourself. Spousal benefits can equal up to 50% of your partner's full retirement amount, depending on when you claim. Survivor benefits are available to widowed spouses, who can receive up to 100% of their deceased partner's benefit. Coordinating these benefits effectively between spouses can maximize the total amount received over a lifetime.

For those who continue working while claiming benefits, it is essential to understand the impact of the earnings test. If you claim benefits before your FRA and continue to work, your benefits may be temporarily reduced based on your income. In 2024, for example, $1 is withheld for every $2 earned above $22,320 until you reach your FRA. Once you reach your FRA, your benefits will be recalculated, and the withheld amounts will be returned in the form of higher payments. To optimize long-term benefits, consider how your earnings interact with Social Security rules and plan accordingly.

Tax considerations also play a significant role in benefit optimization. Social Security benefits may be subject to federal income taxes if your combined income—defined as adjusted gross income, non-taxable interest, and half of your Social Security benefits—exceeds certain thresholds. For individuals, benefits become taxable if combined income exceeds $25,000, and for married couples filing jointly, the threshold is $32,000. Managing your taxable income, such as by timing withdrawals from retirement accounts or utilizing Roth IRAs, can minimize the tax burden on your Social Security benefits and increase your overall financial efficiency.

Another strategy involves accounting for inflation through the Cost-of-Living Adjustments (COLA) applied annually to benefits. While COLA helps to preserve the purchasing power of benefits, relying solely on it may not fully offset the impact of rising costs, particularly for healthcare and housing. Consider supplementing Social Security with other income sources, such as a 401(k), IRA, or annuities, to safeguard against inflation and maintain financial stability over time.

Healthcare expenses are another factor to consider when planning for long-term benefit optimization. Medicare premiums are often deducted directly from Social Security payments, reducing your net benefit amount. Planning for healthcare costs through Health Savings Accounts (HSAs) or other insurance options can help alleviate this burden and ensure you retain more of your Social Security income for other expenses.

Finally, staying informed about legislative changes to Social Security is crucial for long-term planning. Congress regularly debates reforms to address funding shortfalls in the system. Potential changes, such as adjustments to the FRA, benefit formulas, or taxation policies, could impact your benefits. Staying proactive and adjusting your strategy based on new laws or proposals will ensure you maximize your benefits despite a shifting policy landscape.

By implementing these strategies, you can optimize your Social Security benefits and secure a more stable financial future. The key is to start planning early, remain flexible, and adapt to your unique financial and personal circumstances. With careful preparation, Social Security can serve as a reliable foundation for your retirement years.

Chapter 17
Navigating Social Security Changes in 2025 and Beyond

Social Security remains a cornerstone of financial security for millions of Americans, yet it is an ever-evolving program shaped by economic, demographic, and legislative changes. As we move into 2025 and beyond, understanding these changes is crucial for beneficiaries and policymakers alike. This chapter explores the current landscape, the challenges ahead, and strategies to effectively adapt to the evolving system.

One of the most significant developments impacting Social Security in 2025 is the continued demographic shift driven by the aging Baby Boomer generation. Millions of Boomers are retiring each year, leading to a surge in Social Security claims. This influx places immense pressure on the system, as the ratio of workers to beneficiaries continues to shrink. In the mid-20th century, there were approximately 16 workers contributing to Social Security for every retiree. By 2025, that number has dwindled to just over two workers per beneficiary, creating a funding imbalance that threatens the program's long-term solvency.

To address this, policymakers are grappling with a variety of proposals aimed at shoring up the Social Security trust fund. Among these are adjustments to the payroll tax cap, which currently limits taxable earnings at a set amount. Increasing or eliminating this cap could generate additional revenue, helping to sustain the program for future generations. However, such changes face resistance from various political factions, making bipartisan consensus challenging.

Another critical factor influencing Social Security in 2025 is the annual Cost-of-Living Adjustment (COLA). Designed to help benefits keep pace with inflation, COLA adjustments have become a focal point of debate. In recent years, inflation rates have fluctuated dramatically, leading to significant changes in the purchasing power of Social Security benefits. For instance, while beneficiaries saw a record-high COLA in 2023, the adjustment in 2024 was more modest due to cooling inflation. In 2025, COLA is expected to moderate further, which may leave some retirees struggling to cover rising healthcare and housing costs. This highlights the importance of planning for additional income sources to supplement Social Security.

Legislative changes also play a key role in shaping Social Security's trajectory. In late 2024, Congress passed significant reforms repealing the Windfall Elimination Provision (WEP) and the Government Pension Offset (GPO). These provisions had long been criticized for reducing benefits for public-sector workers and their families, often penalizing those who had dedicated their careers to public service. By removing these limitations, lawmakers provided relief to millions of Americans, but the reforms come with financial implications. According to the Congressional Budget Office, the changes are projected to accelerate the depletion of Social Security's trust fund by six months unless offset by new revenue measures or cost adjustments.

For younger workers, Social Security's future looms as an uncertain prospect. While the program is not "going bankrupt," as some alarmist rhetoric suggests, it is clear that adjustments will be necessary to ensure its sustainability. These may include gradual increases to the full retirement age, currently set at 67 for those born after 1960, or changes to benefit formulas that could reduce payouts for higher earners. Policymakers may also explore innovative solutions, such as incentivizing delayed retirement or creating private-public hybrid models to complement traditional Social Security benefits.

In addition to legislative and demographic factors, technological advancements are reshaping the way Americans interact with the Social Security Administration (SSA). In 2025, the SSA is rolling out enhanced online tools to streamline the application process and provide real-time updates on claims. These digital platforms aim to reduce wait times and improve transparency, making it easier for beneficiaries to access the information they need. For those less comfortable with technology, the SSA continues to expand outreach efforts through community centers and partnerships with local organizations.

Looking beyond 2025, Social Security will inevitably remain a focal point of national discourse. The program's challenges are deeply tied to broader economic trends, such as workforce participation rates, wage growth, and the financial health of Medicare, which often intersects with Social Security benefits. As healthcare costs continue to rise, the interplay between these programs will require careful coordination to prevent gaps in coverage for retirees and disabled individuals.

For individuals planning their financial futures, understanding these dynamics is critical. Social Security is designed to be a safety net, not a sole source of income. Therefore, strategies such as contributing to retirement accounts, diversifying investments, and reducing debt remain essential for long-term financial stability. Staying informed about policy changes and periodically reviewing one's Social Security statement can also help individuals make informed decisions about when and how to claim benefits.

As 2025 unfolds, the importance of civic engagement in shaping Social Security's future cannot be overstated. Advocacy groups, unions, and organizations representing retirees continue to play a vital role in pushing for reforms that address inequities while preserving the program's core mission. For beneficiaries, staying involved in these conversations—whether by contacting representatives, attending town halls, or participating in public comment periods—ensures that their voices are heard in the policymaking process.

In conclusion, navigating Social Security changes in 2025 and beyond requires a combination of vigilance, adaptability, and proactive planning. While the program faces significant challenges, it also remains a vital lifeline for millions of Americans. By staying informed, advocating for equitable policies, and planning ahead, individuals can secure a more stable financial future while contributing to the broader effort to preserve Social Security for generations to come.

Conclusion

Social Security remains one of the most essential and transformative programs in American history, providing financial security to millions of individuals and families. As the population ages and economic realities evolve, the significance of this program becomes even more pronounced. For retirees, disabled workers, and survivors, Social Security represents more than just a benefit; it is a lifeline that ensures dignity and support during some of life's most challenging transitions.

Throughout this book, we have explored the intricacies of Social Security—from its historical foundations to its current state and its potential future. Understanding the complexities of the system is the first step toward making informed decisions that can profoundly impact your financial security and peace of mind. By knowing how to navigate the program effectively, you position yourself to maximize the benefits you've earned and safeguard your financial future.

One of the key takeaways is the importance of timing. Deciding when to claim your Social Security benefits can significantly influence the total amount you receive over your lifetime. While it may seem tempting to start collecting benefits as early as possible, delaying your claim can result in larger monthly payments and increased lifetime benefits, especially for those with longer life expectancies. Weighing the trade-offs of early versus delayed benefits requires careful consideration of your financial needs, health, and long-term goals.

Equally important is recognizing how Social Security integrates with other sources of income. Social Security was never designed to serve as the sole source of retirement income; it is meant to complement pensions, savings, and investments. For many, understanding how to blend these income sources effectively can make the difference between financial stability and financial hardship in retirement. The strategies discussed in this book aim to help you develop a comprehensive plan that leverages Social Security benefits alongside your other resources.

Legislation, as we've seen, plays a pivotal role in shaping the future of Social Security. The recent repeal of the Windfall Elimination Provision (WEP) and Government Pension Offset (GPO) illustrates how advocacy and reform can address longstanding inequities in the system. However, with every reform comes challenges, such as funding implications and debates over solvency. As a Social Security beneficiary or future recipient, staying informed about these changes will empower you to advocate for your rights and adapt to new realities.

Cost-of-living adjustments (COLA) remain a cornerstone of Social Security, ensuring that benefits keep pace with inflation. However, COLA adjustments alone may not always match the true cost increases faced by retirees, particularly in healthcare. Being proactive in planning for these discrepancies can help mitigate financial strain and protect your quality of life.

Looking ahead, Social Security faces both opportunities and challenges. The program's long-term solvency depends on decisions made by policymakers and the active engagement of the American public. Proposals to raise the retirement age, adjust payroll taxes, or modify benefits are all on the table. While some changes may seem daunting, they also present an opportunity to strengthen and modernize the program for future generations.

As you reflect on the information shared in this book, consider the broader implications of Social Security on society. It is not just a financial program; it represents a collective commitment to supporting one another through life's uncertainties. By understanding your benefits, advocating for equitable policies, and planning for the future, you contribute to ensuring that Social Security remains a robust and reliable pillar of American life.

In closing, Social Security is a program built on the principles of fairness, equity, and shared responsibility. Its continued success relies on informed individuals who understand its value and advocate for its preservation. Whether you are planning for retirement, navigating current benefits, or exploring options for loved ones, the knowledge you have gained from this guide will serve as a valuable resource.

Your financial future starts with the decisions you make today. Take what you've learned, apply it thoughtfully, and embrace the opportunities to create a secure and fulfilling retirement. Social Security is more than a safety net—it is a foundation for financial independence and stability. With the right approach, you can ensure it works for you and contributes to a future filled with confidence and peace of mind.

www.ingramcontent.com/pod-product-compliance
Lightning Source LLC
Chambersburg PA
CBHW071044250726
48653CB00005B/1994